Table of Contents

Zip The Lip……………………

You're Being F(

Thanksgiving W

Only One Opinic

Through It…………………… 15

The Look……………………… 18

Melting Fear ………………… 21

Sheep Talk…………………… 24

Shortcuts……………………… 27

Open Your Hands…………… 30

No Bad Jobs………………… 33

Mine…………………………… 36

Look Up, Not Around……….. 39

Have A Mercy Christmas……… 42

Grab A Cushion……………… 45

Goofy………………………….. 48

Oh, What a Relief It Is………… 51

Dreams In a Drawer…………… 54

Dear Raymond………………….	57
All Things New………………….	60
Humming………………………..	63
Drive In The Water…………….	66
My Do Not Do List………………	69
Bravehearts…………………….	72
Are You Normal?......................	75
The Smell Test…………………	78
Heartbroken…………………….	81
First steps………………………	84
Because It's True………………	87
Wheelchair Questions…………	90
To Infinity and Beyond…………	93
The Accuser…………………….	96
Bought…………………………..	99
The Blood Never Lies…………	102
Sealed With A Kiss……………	105
Get on the Bus…………………	108
All In Good Taste………………	111
When It Doesn't Add Up………	114

The God of Commas...............	117
Sleep Talking.......................	120
Put Your Hands Together.........	123
Mark My Words....................	126
The will.............................	129
Longing For IT.....................	130
He knows............................	132
The Helpers........................	135

Zip The Lip

Our world has gone mad. Somehow in the name of transparency we think everyone should be honest and open.

I think just the opposite. I believe it is our duty to keep many things to ourselves.

It's called discretion and confidentiality. It's called bridling the tongue. Not every thought needs to be expressed. Not by a long shot.

"He who is a talebearer reveals secrets, but he who is trustworthy keeps a thing hidden." (Proverbs 11:13)

Charles Spurgeon, the great preacher from London, was once criticized for being "offensive". He replied, "You would commend me if you knew what I held back."

What is the goal of the Christian life? The correct answer, of course: "To become more like Jesus."

So what was He like? Let's take a look.

Jesus was asked 307 questions and answered only three directly. He rarely told people who He was.

When he chose to heal, he often told His men to tell no one. A Jerusalem PR firm would have given up in exasperation.

Even in the face of mockery, beatings and crucifixion, "He uttered not a word."

My mom said it well: "You don't need to tell all you know." Many words cause much transgression (Proverbs 10:19). As a speaker, I've found out the hard way.

Too many of us have no off button. Often when I get piecemeal rumors, my tongue-- already set on fire from hell- burns the house down.

Nobody has ever criticized me for keeping my mouth shut. Here's the one that really gets me: "A man of understanding remains silent." (Proverbs 11:12)

We have grown numb to scathing insults and name calling. Razor like words are dividing our country, our homes, our churches, our friendships.

What to do?

Just zip the lip. Let's try standing out by shutting up.

If it's not kind, necessary or true, swallow it. Civility and discretion are still virtues.

How about this option? Talk to God about it. He can handle it.

You think Jesus could have called 10,000 angels while on the Cross? Of course He could. And mowed his accusers down.

Instead He prayed, "Father, forgive them for they know not what they do."

He could have added, "Or what they say."

And when He did talk, He uttered words that made Him our Savior.

"It is finished."

You're Being Followed

My family spent a summer in England in the 1980's. One of our most favorite adventures.

I fell in love with England.

Especially with the traditions among the Royal family. Buckingham Palace. Windsor. The Tower of London. All of it.

I was told, for example, that the Royal Coach that escorted the Queen and King had two small seats in the back.

These were reserved for the Royal Footmen. Two men who stood behind the Coach as it paraded through London.

For some reason, it made me think of Psalm 23.

There is a line at the end of this famous Psalm…"Surely goodness and mercy shall follow you all the days of your life."

Goodness and Mercy.

I think of them now as God's Royal Footmen.

You do know, of course, the Scripture says Believers are part of a Royal Family. We have a King. (I Peter 2:9)

Yet how often we forget — in our spiritual stupor--about our adoption, our royal priesthood, our identity.

We believe it wil all be true in heaven....but now? Not so much.

Yet what gives me great comfort is knowing ;there are two Royal Footmen following me right now. Not just in heaven.

When I can't sleep at night I quote Psalm 23. When I am anxious I read Psalm 23. When I need peace I listen to music about Psalm 23.

I find shalom in this short, vivid, soothing Psalm. I'll wager it will be a go-to refuge for your soul as well.

Memorize it, meditate on it. Say it when you work out. Rise up or go to bed . As you drive. Or fight the monsters at 2 a.m.

Go ahead and personalize the last part. Say it slowly. "Surely Goodness and Mercy WILL Follow ME All the Days of MY life."

Goodness: knowing His plans are always good. Days may be hard. His seasons are good. Hold fast. (I Thessalonians 5:21)

Mercy: knowing He blocks heartache I deserve. So I pray often "Have mercy on me a sinner." (Luke 18:13).

As Believers, even in our loneliest hour we are never alone.

We are Sons and Daughters of the King.
The Privilege of Royalty.
So look behind you.
You're being followed.

Thanksgiving Wonder

I was 10 years old. May 20, 1957. I was shivering with fear in the corner of our Kansas basement, waiting for a killer F5 tornado.

It would forever change 510 lives—dead or injured— and cause millions in damage.

It cut a swath a half mile wide for nearly 100 miles.

I was used to Spring tornados. But this was the Big One.

It skipped passed our home in Lenexa, but as dawn came, we ventured out to see the damage. It was jaw dropping.

Especially hard hit was a town called Ruskin Heights. Their one high school was gone. Only a small brick wall was left.

I'll never forget the letters left hanging on that wall: R-U-I-N. Truer words were never spoken.

Fast forward to today.

Because of my love for Ukraine, I am often asked, what will be left after this devastating war with Russia.

Cities have been ripped apart. Eastern Ukraine is in shambles. Once beautiful cities now rubble. Ruin everywhere.

Of course I don't know. Nobody does. But it reminds me when the armies of Rome laid the land of Israel to waste.

People thought it was over for the Jewish people. But God...

His promise? He would "rebuild the ancient ruins." (Isaiah 61:4) Repair the ruined cities, gather His people to their homeland.

I have long believed that life on this earth is an uneasy blend of wonder over ruin. One day it will all be wonder.

But until then, just like God does, we are called to rebuild the ruins.

God won't give up on Israel. He will keep His promises to His chosen. Despite centuries of rebellion, He won't choose another people.

His heart is always near the broken hearted. (Psalm 34:18). Just like His love for Ukraine. Just like His love for us.

God says when you love someone, and that someone falls apart, you don't abandon . You start to rebuild. Piece by piece.

Restoring what has been broken is called redemption.

He doesn't abandon us in our sins. He doesn't give up on us when we repeat them. He takes the broken parts of our lives and rebuilds.

Here's my hope this Thanksgiving: If you love someone and they're broken…which covers every human still breathing…don't abandon. Rebuild. One life at a time.

Bearing burdens. Patiently enduring. Offering hope.

I'm especially thankful today that Jesus never gave up on me. Instead He rescued me. Redeemed me. Restored me.

And because He is still clearing away the rubble of my F5 mess, replacing my ruin with His wonder...

I will give thanks.

Only One Opinion

Many years ago, a man went to visit a wise old sage.

The man approached the Desert Father and asked, "What do I need to do to be a good leader and a Godly man?"

The wise elder told him, "At the edge of this desert is a cemetery. Go there tonight and spend the night cursing all the graves. Come back the next day."

The man went and did what he was told. The next day, he returned, and the Father asked him, "What did they say?"

"What did they say?" asked the puzzled man. "They didn't say anything. They are all dead."

"Good," says the Father. "Now go back and spend the night praising every grave. Come back tomorrow."

The man returned and the Father asked him, "What did they say?"

"What did they say?" said the man, now frustrated. "They didn't say anything. They're dead."

The old Father looked at the man and said, "When you are dead to both praise and criticism, we can begin…"

"Woe to you when all men speak well of you." Jesus Christ (Luke 6:26)

"Who are you to pass judgment on the servant of another? He stands or falls before his master." Apostle Paul (Romans 14:4)

Judgment or Praise.
In the end...
Only one opinion counts.

Through It

"You might not get over it, but you will get through it."

Words given to me during a tough time.

Are they just a clever play on words? No, there's truth to them.

But there's one word I would add. Believers are **carried** through hard times.

Some of my best memories as a boy were when my father would carry me. His strong hands. A safe place. To a secure rest.

I would even play possum at the end of a long car trip to be carried to bed by my dad.

Our Heavenly Father does the same thing. He really is a Refuge, a Shelter, One who lifts us up. He carries us.

Moses said to a beleagured band of Israelites, "You saw how the Lord your God carried you as a man carries his son (Deut. 1:31)

God carries you as a man carries his son. Such soothing words.

The childfren of God were in a forlorn wilderness. A constant picture of their life. But then becomes a caring and carrying God.

To do the heavy lifting.

One of my biggest unable-to-comprehend moments is when I reflect on God who's surrounded by mighty Angels.

Seraphim and Cherubim cover their eyes and feet because He is holy, holy. (Isaiah 6:2-3). Unable to look, daring not to step too close.

Yet a God who is so tender He reaches down and lifts us up, carrying us through our shadows of death.

The old story is true. When I walk across the sand in my personal desert, I am comforted to see His footprints beside me.

And when I no longer see them, I remember it's when He carried me. He never deserts me in the desert. (Matthew 28:20)

I just helped write a eulogy for a dear friend yesterday who recently lost his beloved brother.

He said his older brother carried him through thick and thin.

As I wrote it, my mind drifted to another time when a Father will carry His son or daughter.

When Believers in Jesus close their eyes for the last time, He carries us from our Wilderness Sand to His Promised Land.

No more getting over it or even through it.

We are carried TO it.

Across the Finish Line.

The Look

My parents had a look for each one of their four boys. My sweet Mom's was mostly an exasperated one.

Yet there was just something magical about her look too.

My dad's look was one of uh-oh, here comes the judge. I think he invented the phrase "if looks could kill."

Normally his was a long stare followed by a quick move--to his belt.

We never knew how he kept his pants up. Fastest move in Kansas. His classic line, "This hurts me more than you."

I always wanted to say, "I know how we could spare you the pain" but something told me to shut up.

Between mom's look and dad's loving spanking, I will tell you what always got to us: it was mom's face.

Her compassionate understanding melted us. It tamed us.

Every Sunday as a kid we used to close our church service with what they called the Benediction. I knew it meant the end was coming. Yes!

I had better things to do than sit on a hard pew for one more minute.

"May the Lord lift up His countenance upon you and give you peace." (Numbers 6:24-26). Last words are lasting words.

I wanted more peace. But had no idea what that fancy word "countenance" meant. Turns out it was His Face. He was looking at me. Gulp.

I immediately thought of my mom. Her look brought me peace.

But because I was guilty most of the time, Jesus looking at me didn't give me much peace.

I read in Sunday school class how Moses went to Mount Sinai and covered His face. Or how He hid His face in the cleft of the rock as God passed by. (Exodus 33:22)

God was so awesome that no one could look at His face and live. I related. I was actually scared of how Jesus looked at me.

Then in college I became a Christian. And everything changed. How?

Well, the first thing I noticed was how I longed to see HIS face.

I no longer wanted to cover MY face. No longer felt the need to hide out. Couldn't wait to meet my Savior face to face.

Now, when He lifts his countenance upon me it does gives me peace. And how you're seen is who you become.

Jesus and my mom.

The Look of Love.

Melting Fear

Seventeen years ago, in a remote part of Nigeria, Africa I was jolted wide awake.

And I wasn't sleeping.

It happened around a campfire late at night when I heard a loud noise in the outer darkness.

I was soon talking to my host, an area Bishop, old and wise beyond his years.

He asked me if I had heard the noise. Well, I wasn't deaf. He seized the teachable moment.

What if that was a hungry lion or a murderer wanting your money? What's the worst thing that could happen to you?

"I guess I could die" I said.

He went on. "What if you were very sick with no cure. What's your worst case scenario?"

"I would die." I was starting to get his point, but he pressed on.

"What if you were fired from your job?" What's the worst thing that could happen to you? He didn't wait for my answer.

"You might starve to death. And if you were a Believer in Jesus Christ what would happen next?"

"I would go to heaven" I said.

Heaven. Just saying the word calmed me.

So, he quietly said, "The worst thing that can happen to you is the best thing that can happen to you."

No more pain. No more sorrow. Fear is gone. Streets of Gold. Unbroken relationships. Unending joy. Perfect Peace.

"So what do you have to be afraid of", he asked "To live is Christ and to die is gain. (Philippians 1:21). Do you believe that?"

He finished talking. But I sensed he still wasn't done.

Finally, he simply said, "Think about that every time fear grips your heart. Perfect Love melts fear." (I John 4:18)...

...And that Perfect Lover lives inside of you."

My campfire lesson was soon to be tested. Two days later, I got news that our grandson Marshall was born.

With five percent lung capacity, barely able to breath. NICU for over 20 days. Me thousands of miles away.

Fear gripped me. Anxiety set in. I too could hardly breathe.

But then I thought, "What's the worst thing that could happen to Marshall?"

He would not need oxygen here. He would breathe the air of Heaven.

I found myself also longing for that pure air of Heaven. I still do.

Able to breathe.

His love melting all my fear.

Sheep Talk

    I was among seven young pastors listening to a wise seminary professor several years ago.

    We were on a weekend retreat when he posed this scenario:

    "One of my students was leading worship in a South America village when suddenly a farmer stood up and said, 'The Lord spoke to me.'

'He told me next week a plague will kill all the cattle in our county. Float your cattle on a raft to the next county or they will die.'

Our retreat leader asked us, "If you were that young pastor what would you do?"

Suddenly, our theology crumbled, searching for a brilliant answer. Instead, we just sat there dumbfounded.

On the next Tuesday, a plague hit the county and all the livestock were killed—except those that floated their herd down stream.

The question behind the story was "Does God speak to His people today?"

Most Christians would say, "Yes...through His Word, through wise counselors, through answered prayer." All true.

But I'm talking about speaking directly TO you. In a still small voice? Maybe in a dramatic loud one? Maybe in a vision?

I used to think He rarely does. I've changed my mind.

I now believe He does. And has. And will. More than we think He does--IF we have ears to hear. (Matthew 11:15)

No, He won't violate His Word. He seldom uses a megaphone. He usually whispers his instructions. But He talks to His sheep.

If He doesn't , I have no clue what "My sheep hear my voice" means. (John 10:27). But we have to clean out the sheep ear wax.

He spoke to the Apostle Paul, he did it thru a farmer in Columbia South America. I believe He'll speak to you.

We do a very poor job of asking the right things. An even poorer job of listening to His voice.

When we boldly approach Him (Hebrews 4:16), Ask 2 questions, "What do you want me to know? What do you want me to do?"

Then perk your sheep ears up.

Here's where I'll go out on a limb. Whatever still small voice comes to your mind, as long as it doesn't oppose Scripture, do it.

He's perfectly capable of re-directing you. The Bible is full of sheep U-turns. You know, we do have a Shepherd.

Five years ago He whispered an idea to me. "Write a small weekly message and call it Salt Talks." Me, a writer? No way.

Two hundred and fifty plus Salt Talks and five books later, here we are.

And here's what's crazy. Know what motivated me to write?

I believed God did speak to a simple farmer when cattle were saved downstream. So why not me? I'm one of His sheep too.

So, fellow lambs, what's the Shepherd saying to you? Ask Him. And when you hear what He's saying, even if it sounds crazy, do it.

Think Noah and the Boat, Jericho and the Walls, Three Boys and the Furnace , Moses and the Sea. Crazy world changing sheep.

What do you have to lose? Fear of failure, looking foolish, being criticized?

Let it be so.

Shortcuts

If you were to win the lottery would you take the lump sum? Or spread it out over time?

Of the past 100 Powerball winners only one chose to to spread it out over 30 years. Ninety nine said "I want my money now."

I recently heard this definition of sin: "Taking a short cut to something God has already promised us." It has a ring of truth.

Take Jesus' temptation in the wilderness. The Lord had fasted forty days and was at His weakest human condition.

Satan appears and offers Him things the Father had already said are His. The devil basically says "Do you want a shortcut?"

Our enemy says the same thing to us. "The future is uncertain. Eat, drink and be merry; for tomorrow you may die."

I'm always wanting the product without the process. Patience without the pain. Triumph without the training.

Shortcuts.

I don't like the long road of the unseen, unknown, usually unappreciated. The work done in the dark. Slowly and patiently.

I've always loved the thrill playing in the big ballgame. Not too keen about the grueling practices.

Sure, celebrate milestones. But it's the sum of moments that matter.

The nation of Israel needed a place to worship after the exile. They were told to rebuild the Temple. The task seemed overwhelming. The work stalled.

Along comes a prophet named Zachariah who says, "Do not despise small beginnings for the Lord rejoices to see the work begin."

Even if it takes 20 years, which it did, keep at it. Brick by brick.

Every New Year's Day I promise myself I will read through the Bible in one year.

I get through Genesis. Binge on Exodus. Then leave it in Leviticus.

Did you know you can read the whole Bible in one year in about 70 hours? Fifteen minutes a day totals 90 hours in a year. Time left over to celebrate.

Note to self: To say I don't have enough time is not a statement of fact, it's a statement of value. We all have 24 hours in a day.

What counts is consistency, not intensity.

We live in a world addicted to the immediate. Neither Rome nor Temples were built in a day.

So when our patience and perseverance wear thin, and they will...let's remind ourselves it's always been about small beginnings.

Then hand me another brick.

Open Your Hands

When I was a kid my dad used to play a game with me I loved.

Out of the clear blue he would say, "Close your eyes and open your hands."

I don't recall one time I disobeyed that request. He always gave me a surprise that delighted my childlike soul.

A piece of candy, a small miniature car, a pack of baseball cards. Little gifts from him.

Or a baseball glove, a BB gun, a KC Royals cap. Larger gifts from him.

Whatever he handed me I would eagerly take. He was my father and I trusted him.

I always had a surge of anticipation. I even squeezed my eyes closed with a tight squinch.

As I grow older, I think this is a good picture of living by faith.

Let's face it. I live my life on this earth with unclear vision. I don't know what tomorrow brings. I see thru a glass darkly. (I Cor. 13:12)

What I think I understand, I rarely do. If life is a mystery to be lived, not a puzzle to be solved, I only have a couple of pieces and no picture on the puzzle box.

I believed to see, I did not see to believe. Jesus Christ lived, rose from the grave, and is coming again. I believed because it's true.

Since that moment in 1969, He simply says "now open your hands." Our Heavenly Father is the God of all surprises.

He hands out things I don't deserve. Call it grace.

He hides the ones I do deserve. Call it mercy.

He gives me things I don't understand. Call it providence.

Faith is coming to God with blurry vision, but open hands.

He says ALL things I give or withhold are for your good. (Hebrews 11)

Like my earthly father, all I need to do to delight my heavenly Father is to give thanks for the gifts. (I Thessalonians 5:18)

Gifts like relishing a hot cup of coffee, a great book, a needed hug, a note of encouragement, a child's laugh. Little gifts from Him.

And count it all joy when we receive different kinds of gifts: a cancer diagnosis, a job layoff, a prodigal kid, a financial reversal. (Romans 8: 28-30, James 1: 2). Larger gifts from Him.

In the end, faith is knowing He is a loving Father who delights in saying "Now close your eyes... open your hands."

And trust Me.

No Bad Jobs

Sometimes you just have to eat crow. Pass the salt and let's talk.

For 30 years I've given a message on finding your calling.

I've said there is a vast difference between a job, a profession and a calling.

As though the value of your job rode in first class, coach or on a jump seat. I take it back. I am announcing I was flying off course.

Here's what I believe now: Your job is wonderful. Even if it's terrible.

I recently read about a guy who was depressed about his job. He sold toilet paper. He tells his story...

"After a meeting in Venezuela, I was riding to the airport. I hear a passenger in my cab say, 'I think I know why people here are so irritable? The toilet paper feels like sand paper.'

Suddenly, he said, "I felt like a missionary with a cause."

Whether you are waiting tables, flipping burgers, mopping floors, or cleaning up poop in a horse stall--you are serving others. Adding value to their lives.

Serving people is not demeaning. It is ennobling. I think it could even be an act of worship.

I just saw the trash truck roll by my office window. Thank goodness for those hard working garbage collectors. I admire you all.

.

I'm working on my taxes now. My CPA actually told me not long ago, "I keep you out of jail." Thank you.

You work at McDonalds? Thank you for feeding our 12 grandkids.

Work is not a result of the Fall. It's not punishment. It was part of Eden's perfection. We need work to thrive. Not just stay alive.

If I ever stop working, I will start to go crazy. I mean it. Even my hobbies are a part of my need to work. God frowns on laziness.

For three decades I have misunderstood the word calling. I was giving out a 3 part formula for finding it. Here's what I said....

"You want to do it, you have the talent to do it, and you see an opportunity to do it." Not wrong. Just utopian.

I was fueling dissatisfaction in the work they were already doing.

So what IS our calling? We have only one. Believers are called to follow Jesus. Simple yet profoundly true. That's our job.

"Whatever you do, work with all your heart, working for the Lord, not for human masters." (Colossians 3: 23-24).

It's not about a position or a paycheck. It's about a Person. Stop looking for the perfect job in God's Providence. It doesn't exist.

Does Jesus care what we do in our vocation or avocation? Maybe, I don't know. I know He cares why we do it.

It's like two bricklayers building a church. One says he's a laborer stacking bricks.

One says he's a stonemason building a magnificent cathedral.

It all depends on Who we call Boss.

Mine

Our precocious and precious grandson Sam has a habit that makes my heart melt.

You might think it's only because I'm partial to anything our 12 grandkids do. Maybe you're right.

But Sam says something that has hit me afresh this Christmas.

Here's how he talks about his father John: "My dad says....My dad gave me...My dad showed me...My dad does that."

I have never heard him refer to his Dad without "My" in front of it. Why does that push an emotional button deep in my soul?

It's how he says MY with such pride.

I was pondering that this morning and I think I know why it tenderizes me. The word "my" is both profound and simple.

It's like I'm supposed to live as a Believer. God is profound and I am simple. And I am increasingly so at peace with that.

The Lord is MY Shepherd, I shall not want. The joy of the Lord is MY strength. God is MY refuge and shield. The Lord is MY help in time of need.

I have everything I need because He is mine. It's as simple yet profound as that.

There are 32 Names for God in the Bible in the Hebrew language. They may mean: Powerful. Sovereign. Omnipotent. Provider. Healer. Deliverer.

The most comforting one for me? Adonai. It means MY God.

My Jesus isn't a far-off God-Man who lets me run from Him, afraid of His wrath. He runs towards me as a Father runs with compassion to His Prodigal son.

He says Draw close to Me. (James 4:8). Taste and see that I am Good. (Psalm 34:8) Come to me, all you who are weak...and I will give you rest." (Matthew 11: 28).

Abide with me. Stay near. I want your company. The creator of the Universe wants my company? Staggering!

Yes, He is to be feared as a Holy God. Yes, He judges our rebellion. Enter the Cross. The Easter Message. The Story of Forgiveness.

So we can say like Thomas, "MY Lord and MY God."

But the Baby in a manger says, "Emmanuel, God is with us." The Christmas Message. The Story of Love.

So, listen carefully how a Christian says, "My Jesus." It tells you all you need to know.

Like MY grandson Sam would say...wide eyed, proud and grateful...

My Abba.

Look Up, Not Around

I am thinking about unveiling a new approach to determine personality types.

Forget the Myers-Briggs or Enneagrams. I think we ought to have a Peanuts Profile.

Are you a Lucy or a Sally? A Linus or a Charlie Brown? Maybe even a Schroeder?

I am definitely a Charlie Brown. I cause a lot of people to say "rats" or "Good Grief Charlie Brown!"

I grew up loving the comic strip Peanuts. My best growing up friend was Linus, my favorite Philosopher/Theologian.

The comic strip filled me with childlike wonder. Made me grateful for simple things. Unfortunately, I lost that along the way.

I think the Apostle Paul and cartoonist Charlie Schultz would agree: Gratitude and Anger cannot coexist.

One drains life from you. One fills life with meaning.

Pick one or the other. As an emotional Charlie Brown, I don't often pick gratitude. Turns out I have a quick fuse.

I complain about politics, gripe about things out of my control, get swept up in injustice.

What has happened to me? Trust and obey has become stinkin' thinkin'. I can hear Linus say "Look up, not around."

"As a man thinks, so he is." (Proverbs 23:7)

I already know this world is broken. I know we are asleep at the wheel. I also know that He alone holds it all together—and He's wide awake.

When I look around instead of up, I get caught up in my much smaller, deadening story. I only know part of the Bigger Story.

Anger or gratitude. The choice is mine. Where do I get the power to choose?

I camp on one truth when I am sick of it all: God's goodness. It's the deepest reality I know.

No purpose of His can be thwarted. (Job 42:2) Not in elections, not in wars, not in my bad decisions, not my work, not even in my sin.

Pondering His Goodness pins my ungrateful, angry heart to the mat.

There is a Linus exercise that helps my Charlie attitude.

He prays two words when he gets up in the morning: Help Me!

And two words before he goes to bed: Thank You!

Wise words from the Peanut Gallery.

Linus knew God never gave anybody a critical spirit.

Good Grief, Linus...Hand me your Blanket.

Have A Mercy Christmas

I was 10 years old and I remember my dad putting down a dime as a tip for a cup of coffee.

Right then and there I knew I wanted to be a waiter. Can you imagine? Five cents for coffee and double that for a gratuity.

I actually said to my father, "You accidentally left a dime on the table!" I saw my penny candy allowance going up in smoke.

When my father explained what he was doing, I thought "I have a very very rich dad."

Have you ever tried to define the word rich? When do you become rich? How much is enough? I don't know.

But did you know there is only one place in all the Bible where God is described as rich? Only one.

"God, being rich in mercy...". (Ephesians 2:4). It's His Mercy.

He doesn't just show mercy. He doesn't become merciful. His very nature IS mercy.

And not only that: He DELIGHTS in giving mercy. (Micah 7:18). He loves lavishly giving it away.

God is a multi-billionaire in mercy currency and His vast fortune is forever being poured out to us.

When He answers with delight my constant prayer, "God have mercy on me a sinner", He is just being Himself.

Think about it. God is just and holy, sovereign and good. He is love. But He is RICH in mercy.

Why? Ephesians 2:4 continues, "because of the great love He has for us."

Mercy means He holds back what we deserve. And gives us what we don't.

To me, it means when I squander His mercy by one stupid decision or 1000 little ones, He pours out more.

His supply is inexhaustible.

As one person puts it, "Mercy means the things that make us cringe the most, makes Him hug the hardest."

When we stand before Him one day, we will weep with relief. Stunned at how shallow we saw His mercy.

I recently read a letter from a friend who signed off with "Under the Mercy." At the time I was listening to "Oh Come Let us Adore Him."

This Christmas I am so thankful I am Under the Mercy. Adoring Him is all I can do in response.

It reminds me what I said to my earthly dad 67 years ago, "I have a very, very rich Father." And a generously merciful One too.

Have a Very Mercy Christmas!

Grab A Cushion

    I returned recently from an out of the country trip and was exhilarated.
    In every sense it had been a success.
    Then I crashed.
    I went from the penthouse to the outhouse.
    Initially my doctor thought maybe pneumonia, and told me to head to the hospital. After several tests the verdict came in…

I had the flu.

My first thought was "Just the flu?" I thought I was dying and then I wanted to. Miserable to my toenails.

If people tell you they THINK they have the flu, they don't. You will know it.

The phrase "I couldn't raise my head off the pillow" is no joke. I rotated for 10 days from one bed to two couches.

Lost 9 pounds and food tasted like cardboard. So what did I learn?

Sleep is a bigger deal than I thought. I'm a big fan.

I was never a nap taker. Naps are now in. I claim the promise God works even as I sleep. (Psalm 127:1)

When He wants you to lie down in your green pasture, you will go down. In fact, Psalm 23 says He makes you lie down. Boy, does He ever.

I kept thinking about the famous passage where Jesus is asleep on a cushion as a storm rages on the Sea of Galilee.

I began to see Him sleeping in the midst of chaos in a different light. The creator of the Universe is calm. His disciples are anything but.

With a word he wakes up and calms the storm HE allowed. My endless flu-induced-sleep reminded me He is God and I am not. My to do list will remain undone.

When chaos comes, just like King David, we can say "I lie down and sleep because the Lord sustains me, even though thousands attack me." (Psalm 3: 5-6)

David tells us why he can sleep one Psalm later, "In peace I will sleep, for I dwell in your safety."

He's where my help comes from (Psalm 121:2). He fights my battles (Exodus 14:14). He is my refuge. He is my shelter. (Psalm 91:2). He is my strength (Psalm 73:26).

As I fretted with the flu, some of these words came drifting back: He really does holds me safely.

He's not surprised at my storm. He's behind my storm. He will calm my storm.

My job? Remember Who's in the boat with me.

.

My favorite all time message describing Jesus asleep during the Storm concluded with these words:

...The boat will not sink and the storm will not last forever...

So whether it seems fatal or forever.... Or the annoying flu.

Grab a cushion. Close your eyes. And sleep.

You're in Good Company.

Goofy

Know any narcissists? Guess what they simply cannot do?

Laugh at themselves. It's almost impossible for them to have fun.

You know when my faith looks weird? Even creepy? When I try to make it look cool.

Being cool is a trap. Smoothness is way overrated. It's because religion always smells funny.

Being open to look like a fool is freeing. What else could it mean when we are urged to be a fool for Christ's sake? (I Corinthians 4:10)

What else could it mean when God says "in your weakness I am made strong." (II Corinthians 12:9)

Most people think they grow out of awkwardness by high school. They haven't. We adults are just better at faking it.

Awkward-goofy could reflect a life of childlike faith and vulnerability-- along with a lighthearted humility.

People don't need smooth. They need friends. And deep friendships are formed around vulnerability. Without pretense.

When I am temporarily impressive, guess who gets the credit. I do.

When God works through my faltering, embarrassing, wanna-get-away moments, guess who does? He does. And that's a good thing.

I have laid an egg while teaching, run into shut patio doors at full speed, had my zipper open preaching on Easter morning.

I've had dinner rolls thrown at me while speaking at banquets, committed three errors in one inning in Class A pro ball (still a record).

The list could go on and on. At my age, the show's over. I almost expect being goofy. I have it down to an art form.

Courting admiration is both fleeting and a heavy burden. It's exhausting.

So how has accepting goofiness changed me?

Well, I try new stuff. If I look like an idiot, so what? If I fail at a new idea, par for the course. I laugh more at myself.

Nothing to prove, nothing to lose.

It's because I really do believe Psalm 23:1 is true. I am one of his sheep, He is my Shepherd. I shall not want.

So... go for it. Times to be serious? Of course. More times to laugh at myself? Yes. Best times? When we're all laughing together..

I swear our marriages would be better off, our faith more attractive, our attempts to cover up fewer.

I suddenly have an idea. Let's start a new movement. Christian Celebrities are not allowed to join.

Lets call it Goofballs for God.

Oh, What a Relief It Is

One of my favorite actors growing up was Andy Griffith, a very gifted performer who worked his magic for 70 years.

I took great delight in touring his museum in Mount Airy, NC. The town was a replica of Mayberry.

While I loved Opie, Aunt Bee, and Barney, my favorite show was Matlock, where Andy played a crafty lawyer who, like Perry Mason, rarely lost a case.

Well, recently there was a resurrection of Matlock, starting Kathy Bates as Matlock. She is terrific in this remake.

What I didn't know about Kathy until this past week was for over 30 years she carried of boatload of guilt.

It seems that when Kathy won an Oscar in 1991, she failed to thank her mother in accepting the award.

Her mother called her on it and for three decades it ate at her. And her mother always reminded her of the oversight.

During a recent interview, Kathy was questioned about it. Her face told the story with regret.

Then came the revelation. The interviewer told her she actually DID thank her mother that night. Kathy scornfully denied it.

But sure enough, as Kathy watched a replay of her speech, she did thank her mother. It was a poignant moment.

As Kathy watched the clip, her eyes got big, she gasped, and through tears said in a soft voice, "Oh, what a relief."

Thirty three years of guilt and shame vanished. The camera did not lie.

Mark Twain said, "It is easier to fool people than to convince them they have been fooled."

I think we all buy lies. In Kathy Bate's mind she was sincere, but sincerely wrong.

For the Believer, there are only two sources of truth: The Written Word and the Living Word.

Your Word is Truth. The Bible. (John 17:17) I am the Way, the Truth and the Life. (John 14:6). Jesus Christ.

All of us are prone to believing half-truths: whether from our well meaning parents, a favorite preacher, or best selling book.

False teachers? Peter takes us to the Word. Denial of Christ's Deity? John takes us to the Word. A "new" doctrine vs. a timeless truth? Paul takes us to the Word.

Here's the reality: most Christians don't know their Bible. And only His Truth will set us free. (John 8:32). Start by vowing to read it thru in 2025. Get a plan. Any plan.

The Word of God is better than any opinion, no matter how it makes us feel, how much we are convinced, or how logical it sounds.

Only when we surrender to the truth of the Bible giving us the truth about Jesus…as Kathy Bates would say...

"Oh, What a Relief."

Dreams In a Drawer

As a kid, I remember crying myself to sleep over two movies: Peter Pan and Old Yeller.

One of the conversations in the book *Peter Pan* is astounding. It's between young Michael and his mother Mrs. Darling...

Mrs Darling: "There are different kinds of bravery. Your father has never used a sword or pistol. But he thinks of others before himself.

He's made many sacrifices for his family and put away many dreams."

Michael: "Where did he put them?"

Mrs. Darling: "He puts them in a drawer. And sometimes, late at night, we take them out and admire them.

It gets harder and harder to close the drawer. But he does. And that's why he's brave."

Don't you just love that? Brave indeed.

It's my new description of bravery in a world of self-promotion: being brave enough to close the drawer of your dreams.

Our Western idea of freedom is first seen in the Fall of Genesis 3. Get all you can, ignore the boundaries. It's actually rooted in selfishness.

I think pure bravery is putting your dreams in a drawer for the sake of others.

Chasing after your dreams is cheap compared to the cost of giving your life away. Yes. It says easy, does hard.

"Not my will but Your will be done." (Luke 22:42)

I read a sign outside a crisis pregnancy center that said, "You can have your dreams and your babies too."

Although well intentioned, I think it's rarely true. Many of our dreams are prone to die with new life in the delivery room.

Babies tend to change our bucket list. Life becomes, well, messy.

And let's face it. Dreams die hard. I get it. The lure of achievement has pulled at my heart strings all my life.

So early in my morning, I often open my dream drawer and think what might have been. I sigh.

I don't think that makes me selfish. It makes me human.

But at my age, and with God's grace, I shut the drawer.

Then I pause and think. I have a family that loves me. Grandkids that tolerate me. A fulfilling ministry. A church I love. Men who share life with me.

I've seen the world. Failed often. Been forgiven much. Often criticized. More often encouraged.

And because Jesus set aside HIS dreams, I am going to heaven.

When I shut the drawer where dreams go to die, I am struck by a far bigger truth than any regret.

Dying to dreams in my drawer has allowed me to clarify my reality.

What's that?

I really am living the dream.

Dear Raymond

I've never been showered with so much attention. I guess I should feel loved.

Who says this is a cancel culture? I just erased 146 emails from Kamala and Donald.

One addressed me as Randolph and the other pegged me as Raymond.

The "election of our lifetime" desperately needs my $47 dollars.

See how specific I feel loved? No rounding it up to $50 bucks. No sir.

How did they know that's exactly what I have left in my checking account?

Although their appeals "end at midnight tonight", I'll betcha If I gave tomorrow I could still help change the course of history.

I think we're all counting the days until the results are in. How do you spell relief? O-V-E-R.

I grew up in a political family. My dad was mayor of our town for a long time…"Be Partial Vote Marshall" was our cry.

All the boys in the family went door to door campaigning for my father.

Dyed in the red Republican, the thought of any of us voting Democrat was akin to ripping up the Constitution.

My goal? To become a US Senator. My reality? I became a Christian and moved into big time politics.

I became a pastor.

It was there I learned God "changes the seasons, removes kings and establishes kings." (Daniel 2:21)

It was there I discovered the same God who created 200 billion trillion stars "calls them each by Name." (Psalm 139:13-16)

It was there I learned "no purpose of His can be thwarted." (Job 42:2)

It was there I found out "the nations are like a drop in a bucket. And are regarded as a speck of dust on the scales." (Isaiah 40:15)

It was there I learned I can relax in how He handles Donald and Kamala. Or me. Or you.

Like the rest of us, both candidates will take a knee to the King of Kings and Lord of Lords one day. (Philippians 2: 10–11)

The only poll that counts then is whether our names are written in the Book of Life. (Luke 10:20)

So please do vote for the elephant or the donkey. But In the end, we're all voting for the Lion and the Lamb.

Or not.

By the way, I also learned I'll get a new name in Heaven. (Revelation 2:17).

I kinda hope it's Raymond.

Everybody Loves Raymond.

All Things New

When I was a kid I loved a new book, a new bike, a new lunch box, a new friend, a new song.

I loved buying a new 5 dollar wooden bat in the Spring—preferably a magical one full of hits.

We all want a fresh start. I always liked baseball more than football. Why?

Because I didn't have to wait a week to get over my miserable performance the day before. We'd often play the next day.

I wanted a do-over. Don't we all?

My hope and prayer as we flip the calendar? Please let this be the year the Lord Jesus returns for His own.

And brings with Him a New Earth. A return to a New Garden of Eden. EVERYTHING made brand spanking new--as it once was.

He who is seated on the throne will say, " I am making everything new." (Revelation 21: 4--5)

A Do-Over.

All suffering reversed. Sin banished forever. Rewards bestowed to the faithful. The Banquet Table covered with culinary perfection.

ALL things new!

.

Nursing children playing with rattlesnakes. Toddlers with serpents. The Lion and the Lamb lying down together.

Tears will vanish. Death defeated. Mountains clapping. Colors exploding. Like it was always supposed to be.

As we live on the precipice of a New Year with so many things coming unglued…pause and try to FEEL NEWNESS coming for a moment. Grasp it in child like wonder.

As the old song says, "I can only imagine." But really do try.

Does it make you feel like King David dancing in his underwear before the Ark of the Covenant? (2 Samuel 6:14—22)

Does it make you feel like Fiddler on the Roof, leaping from housetop to housetop? Or Scrooge happily running around on Christmas Day?

For me, it feels like something so tender my soul can barely stand it. At last I will be made complete, wholehearted, goodness flowing from head to toe.

My splintered soul in this groaning body will finally be restored, renewed, rescued. Released!

Today reminds me again "Old things have passed away, behold all things have become new." (2 Corinthians 5:17).

Be assured of this fellow Believer: A deliriously Happy New Year will come soon, when there will be no shame, no doubt, no lust, no regret. Come quickly Lord Jesus!

Join me in toasting 2025- the year of the Do-Over.

I Can Only Imagine.

Humming

I can always tell when I am doing OK spiritually. I listen to music, I read books… and I hum.

Yup—I hum. I know it's weird. But so be it. I have a lot of weird habits. For example?

I don't put other books on top of the Bible when I stack books. I tap a painting of Aslan every morning and say good morning to the mighty Lion.

I really have strange habits. So do you—so don't look at me with that tone of voice.

But…I am now announcing this morning that I may not be so weird after all. Why? I have found something more strange than me.

I am reading through Bible in one year and I've almost finished the book of Leviticus. There is no stranger compilation of writ in the Galaxy.

All I can say is I'm glad I wasn't a Jew being asked to know, let alone follow, the requirements of a Holy God. 251 laws in the book!

The regulations to please a God who is perfect is staggering, puzzling and, well, impossible.

I did not hum once as I read each chapter.

Here is my conclusion: God at no time, in any way, thinks like I do.

From leprosy, to diet, to sanitary requirements, to killing animals, to lots of blood, to bodily discharges—it is overwhelming.

That Moses could remember all that the Lord commanded, let alone expect Aaron the High Priest to pull it off is beyond belief.

Sure…it points to a Messiah that fulfills all of the law's requirements. It causes me to bow in adoration to the One who paid the price by bridging the gap between us and a Holy God.

Yes, this was a new nation to be holy (set apart) unlike all the other idol-fearing, god chasing nations.

Here's what jumped off page after page and caused me to start humming again.

Four words: 49 times after the command to bring animals, the blood and food as temple offerings, God says. "I AM THE LORD."

Meaning to me: He says what He means and means what He says. The problem? I, along with eight billion people fall woefully short. "Be holy for I am holy…." Good luck with that.

The answer? A New Sacrifice, A New Temple, A New High Priest. Who could it be?

The different altar? An old Cross. A thick Veil? Torn in two. The Proof? An Empty Tomb. Who could it be?

My only Hope: Jesus Christ… Our New Temple, Our New Priest, Our New Sacrifice. Once and for all. Dead and raised to Life. It is Him!

My childlike part? Simply believe His Promise….. (John 6:47)

Old things have passed away—a New Song has come!

I will forever hum to that song.

Like a hummingbird set free.

Drive In The Water

There is a family camp in the Texas Hill Country called Laity Lodge.

After winding around beautiful terrain at the headwaters of the Frio River, you come to a sign at water's edge, which says, "Yes, you drive in the water."

You have to drive thru the river to get to the lodge.

You feel like one of the Hebrews marching behind Moses as he raises his staff at the Red Sea and announces, "Yes, you walk through the water."

Every Believer will eventually come to a dangerous looking river. It looks impossible to cross. We glance around for an alternative route. There is none.

You can't see the bottom of the river. It rained the night before. How deep is it now? You think "Well, others must have crossed before me." Analysis doesn't help.

With an cascade of emotion, all you really know is that God wants you to get to the lodge.

As one knee says to the other, let's shake, you quote from Deuteronomy, "The Lord your God will cross over with you. He will not fail you nor forsake you. Do not be discouraged or afraid."

It doesn't help. You quote every Bible verse on anxiety you know. Still no surge of faith.

I have been on stuck at water's edge so many times: Lost on mission trips. Entrapped by my own rebellion. My comfort zone crushed. Feelings trumping faith.

At times I've echoed Esher's declaration of courage: "If I perish, I perish." Most times, I've wanted to turn around and drive back, gripped by fear.

A helpful story for me is told by an old Scottish Preacher. A woman came to him fighting a very human temptation, knowing the Bible clearly said to do the opposite.

The pastor wrote two two words on a slip of paper. Handed the paper to her and told her to ponder it for 10 minutes and cross out one of the words.

She sat down and read: "No Lord". She quickly understood. If she crossed out Lord, she was saying "I'm not going to do what You ask."

If she crossed out No, she was left with only the Lord… what He wanted her to do. And maybe an unknown river-crossing.

Sure there are lots gray areas in life, needing wisdom. We navigate the gray prayerfully. At times He even carries us across the river.

But there are more times I simply need to obey what is clear…period. I'm left only with the Lord, to increase my faith and cross the river. Do what is hard. What is scary.

My prayer? Help me when I don't know how deep the water is---but I know Who made the river... and Who posted the sign.

I have a wise friend who says you can sum up the Christian life in three words. "Trust and Obey." I think he's right.

John H. Sammis penned a hymn I sang as a baby Christian. I sing it now as old weathered one: "To be happy in Jesus there is no other way but to trust and obey."

Want happiness? Trust and obey.

Release the brakes. Press the pedal. Drive in the water.

There is no other way.

My Do Not Do List

Ever had one of those days when everything looks gray? Nothing really wrong. It all just seems so blah.

It's like when I get ready for bed, I say to myself, "Didn't you JUST do this?"

I'm having one of those days. My mood has been super reflective. Everything spiritual I read seems so predictable and religious...and frankly boring.

I sat down to write a Salt Talk and the computer stared back at me with a smug, give-it-up attitude. Nothing salty about it.

Downright meh.

During times like this, I have been tempted to just "do something."

You know, shake off the cobwebs and go be with people. Try and give a blessing to receive a blessing. Play my favorite music on repeat. Listen to an inspring speaker.

Something to shake the ho-hum doldrums.

Early this morning I had an epiphany. Here's what I have decided to do: Nothing.

I am officially turning my To Do List into my Not To Do list. I'm tempted to wear sweat pants and a hoodie all week.

And in honor of my not feeling accomplished, productive, or energetic…I have devised a Don't Do It List.

Here are three of them:

1) Don't overpromise when you're happy. (Matthew 5:37)

2) Don't reply when you're angry. (Proverbs 15:18)

3) Don't decide when you're sad. (James 1:19)

Instead of ready, aim, fire I am adopting a different strategy this week: sit, soak, simmer.

Just reflect. You know, try being a Mary at the feet of Jesus.

As in, "Be still and Know I am God". (Psalm 46:10) I'm putting the never-ending To Do list on hold. It will be there when I get back.

My showers will be slower. Gonna have a second/third cup of coffee. Chew my food and taste it. Read a brainless book about my fave comedian Steve Martin.

When I overpromise because I'm happy, react when I'm angry, or make a decision when I'm down…I invariably regret it.

So please excuse me for being a downright yawn this morning. My Salt Talk has turned into a Slow Walk.

I'll let you know how my unproductive, do-not-do-list, zero hero week turns out.

I'm sure I'll feel guilty.

I'll do my best to get over it.

Bravehearts

Recently I attended our grand daughter Annie's cheerleading competition where thousands of kids were performing.

Our daughter in law Julia, a former University of Alabama cheerleader, teaches cheerleading and has a wait list.

What's the deal with cheerleading?

I am a huge believer that everyone needs a cheerleader. Bringing big doses of encouragement.

It's so easy to lose heart in this cynical, negative, upside down world.

"And let us not lose heart...". Galatians 6:9. "Therefore do not lose heart...". II Corinthians 4: 16—18. "Let not your hearts be troubled...". John 14:1.

When I lose heart I lose courage. Interestingly, the word courage comes from the root word heart. What happens when we lose heart?

We shrink back. We become passive. We are swept along. We sigh with quiet desperation.

I loved the movie Braveheart. Turns out, I'm not alone. I think all of us want to have brave hearts. To not shrink back.

We all want a bit of William Wallace: to be brave in the face of fear. To show courage. Not lose heart.

So how can I find my brave heart when I am feeling lost, overwhelmed, feinting?

Just as important, how can I help find the courage to cheer others on to the Finish Line?

Well, at the risk of what sounds easy-- but is not-- here's mine. I am reading my Bible. Reading my Bible. Just reading it.

Too simple you say? Sounds simple but does hard.

I have started a "read thru the Bible in One Year" program.

So I am a bit embarrassed to admit this...But--

I have gone to seminary, taught at one, pastored, and it's like I am reading Scripture for the first time.

I feel like a kindergarten teacher just handed me a copy of "Run, Spot, Run."

I never realized there was so much weirdness in the first 22 chapters of Genesis. In just four days, I feel staggeringly ignorant.

Yet a strange thing is happening. After I read it, I seriously feel stronger of heart. More brave. And a renewed desire to cheer others on.

So here's a thought for the New Year...forget trying to understand your Bible. Sure, give it your best shot.

But just jump in. It's living and powerful. Let it have its own way. The Spirit's job is to steel our hearts with bold courage.

In the mysterious ways of God, I believe He will give us a braver heart. If you feel stale, bored, listless, dive in with me.

William Wallace was right. "All men die, but not all men really live." Let's unsheathe the sword in 2025 (Hebrews 4:12). The Year of the Word.

And let it revive our hearts, cheer us on, give us courage!

Make us brave.

Are You Normal?

I'm staring out my second story office at the snow, now melting after a 24 hour wintry mix that dropped a whopping two inches.

Everything may be bigger in Texas, but when it comes to facing frozen water we are a bunch of wimps.

My friends in Kansas City and St. Louis laugh at us, as they get 12 inches of snowfall and fight rush hour traffic.

I haven't heard a peep of cars crunching snow all day.

Texans have normalized their fear of snow. For Canadians, this would be beach weather.

So what's my point?

As Watchman Nee puts it, "Christians have exchanged normal for average." In other words, we have normalized average.

We live in unique bubbles. Biible Belt style, Denominational style, West Coast style, Charismatic style. The familiar can morph into average. Same language, same routine.

We get along by going along. What we call contentment is really complacency. We begin to measure our Christian life by looking around, not up.

"Do not be conformed to this world, but be transformed by the renewing of your mind"...(Romans 12:1). We are being squeezed into a mold.

The normal Christian life is radical. The average Christian life is religious. By radical, I don't mean being weird, loud, obnoxious. Jesus doesn't make you weird.

But He does make you radically normal. And dangerous in the eyes of the religiously safe bubble-dwellers.

I believe Americans are increasingly becoming average in our faith, and increasingly impotent in our impact.

And worst of all: we still smugly proclaim we are a Christian nation of Salt and Light.

I thought I was heaven's gift to baseball in college--then I played for the KC Royals organization. My hot stuff became average. I needed a new normal. So do we.

We have lost the edge because we have lost the benchmark of normal. Tasteless salt, often bored, we float along in religious bubbles.

Our faith has become insulation rather than transformation. A conformed huddle rather than holy trouble.

As I now look out my window, I see the Sun starting to melt the ice.

Jesus the Son also came to melt the ice. To transform icy average hearts into hot normal change agents.

So what's the first step in thawing the Frozen Chosen? Simply being convinced God wants us to be normal, not average.

Are you normal?

If so, good. You're looking up.

Are you average? Stop looking around.

And pop some religious bubbles.

The Smell Test

I'm watching the show The Mentalist now, a long running, old fashioned detective show.

Patrick Jane, the star of the show, has a very strange way of examining a murdered body. He first smells them.

He's smelling for clues. How bizarre is that?

When my mom didn't like a friend I brought home, she would say, "He doesn't pass the smell test." She was also looking for clues.

Turns out, so is God. He's into sniffing us to find a pleasant aroma. Finding clues of life in us.

I cannot believe how many times the phrase "sacrifice a pleasant aroma to God" is mentioned in the Old Testament.

Lo and behold, it's mentioned a lot in the New Testament too.

I have a theory: the closer we get to Jesus, the better we smell. To God and to others.. Our aroma gives off unmistakable odors.

I remember very pleasant occasions and recall certain smells.

A wood burning stove at my aunt's dairy farm. Chocolate chip cookies from Grandma Ethel's kitchen. Freshly mowed grass on a baseball field. A new car fragrance. Grandpa's pipe.

It's a good thing as Believers we are no longer bound by OT law— we offer a different kind of smelly sacrifice: not of sheep, donkeys, goats, lambs, pigeons, or cattle. What kind?

You guessed it: we offer ourselves.

Romans 12:1: "Present your bodies on the altar as a living and holy sacrifice...acceptable to God."

2 Corinthians 2:16: "To one we are an aroma who brings life to life. To the other an aroma who brings death to death."

Today the Holy of Holies is not in a Tabernacle made of hands. Christ followers ARE the tabernacle. Unfathomable!

Instead of the Ark of the Covenant, the Believer carries the Holy Spirit in our bodies. We ARE the Temple. Incomprehensible!

So Who is it that gives off a pleasant aroma now? HE does in you and me ...then WE do it for others. (Galatians 2:20).

He has nine different odors: love, joy, peace, patience, kindness, meekness, goodness, faithfulness, self-control. (Galatians 5)

Think of us like a supernatural aerosol can. The only way we smell up the place is by grieving or quenching the Spirit (IThess. 5:19). We plug Him up. We normalize stinky.

How do we unplug? By releasing the good smells of God. Releasing His grace when we smell funny.

Our job is to push the aerosol button.. It's called repentance. His job is to unleash the aroma. It's called the Fruit of the Spirit.

The result? "I accept you as a sweet aroma." (Exekiel 20:41)

We ace the Smell Test.

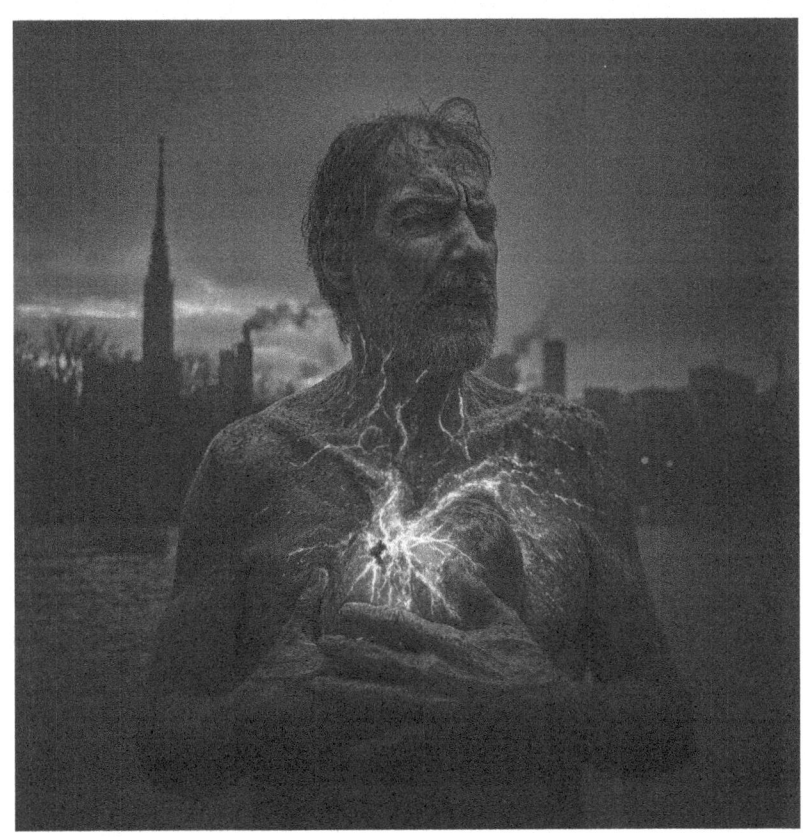

Heartbroken

I started writing Salt Talks over five years ago. I vowed I would never talk politics. I lied. It's time to talk.

I may be out of line, no doubt emotional, but this ongoing political idiocy I take personally. The news about Ukraine is breaking my heart.

I love the people of Ukraine. Since 2010 I have worked there. I was in Lviv 6 days before Russia invaded Ukraine.

Key phrase: before RUSSIA invaded Ukraine. Not the other way around.

Wanna know how to end this war? Dear Russia: pack up your ammo and go home.

Since the invasion, Putin's barbarians have destroyed cities, killed thousands, wrecked the country's economy, and risen to the level of Hitler's terrorism.

The recent actions and comments out of Washington DC have stunned me.

You've read the headlines...and because I am a Christ follower, I will attempt to keep this PG.

I am a patriot...100% American. But what is happening is appalling.

When our leader says Ukraine started this War, then negotiates directly with a madman, demands Ukrainian mineral rights, THEN labels Zalensky, the President of Ukraine, as a dictator is all damaging nonsense.

It's embarrassing to our country, shockingly ignorant—mixed with bullying expediency.

Europe is shocked. My Ukrainian friends feel abandoned. Their soldiers are demoralized. I am angry.

My Salt Talk this morning is a Psalm of Lament. You know, the 50 Psalms that rail at what is happening and suddenly remembers the One who recalibrates hearts.

The One who sees the nations as dust (Isaiah 40:15). The One who puts down one leader and raises up another (Psalm 75:7). The One whose purpose you cannot thwart. (Job 42:2)

The One who reduces leaders to dust (Isaiah 40:23).

Yes, I am mad... but I am more madly in love with the One who is still on the throne. The One who is never caught by surprise. Who knows the beginning from the end.

So what do I do when my friends in Ukraine ask, "Does he think he is a King?" I keep my mouth shut, listen to their frustration... and try to point them to the real King.

I talk about a King coming to make everything new, when all in DC and Moscow-- and Kyiv-- will one day bow the knee.

Just because I don't understand what's going on doesn't mean I get to question the God who does.

It also doesn't keep me from having a broken heart.

Yes, His lovingkindness endures.

So does my outrage.

First Steps

I am doing a fast this week. Evidently I'm supposed to keep it a secret or it loses its spiritual value.

This one is for physical reasons, not spiritual. And I will tell you right now, food never looked so good.

I have finished day two. Those folks that tell you "Oh you'll get used to it" or "it will get easier" are demented.

I like to eat. I really like comfort food. Fasting is not comfortable.

I blocked off days this week with no appointments because I want to save what little Christian witness I have left.

I figure biting someone's head off does not count as righteous indignation.

Mind you, this is not a 40 day fast. The people who are able to do that deserve buildings with their names on them.

But here's what I hope happens....I'll experience change.

I resist change. At my age, I really fight it. I like my routine. But God calls for change, no matter how old I am.

My hope? This first step of fasting will lead to bigger changes. To put it another way, I need to get the ball rolling.

Every change begins with overcoming initial inertia. Something about the law of new momentum.

And the bigger the change, the harder the first step will be. The beginning one will be the most difficult.

It's why you and I don't do it.

When Moses was called by God after 40 years in the wilderness in a burning bush what did He ask him to do?

Take off your sandals. A talking bush knocked him out of his rhythm.

What did Jesus ask his first disciples to do? Follow Me...leave the only profession you've ever known.

They dropped their nets. Now fishers of men?

Both Moses and the Apostles took a stunning, scary first step. And what happened?

They changed--then changed the world.

One of the hardest first steps I ever took was when I attended Regeneration…a one year 12 Step program to deal with hurts, habits and hangups.

I was driving to the initial meeting and literally turned my car around three times.

That first step of just showing up changed my life. It was so hard. The results were so freeing.

I discovered this: What you're not changing, you're choosing.

Let's face it. I hate fasting. Throw a feast and everyone comes; throw a fast and nobody shows up. But...what I hate even worse? Regret.

What are you circling, putting off, knowing you need to take the first step?

The first one is so so hard.

But it might just change the world.

Or change yours.

P.S. I am done fasting as of this Monday morning. My stomach thinks my throat's been cut.

Step Two: Eat.

Because It's True

I am in St. Louis visiting some dear friends. I asked our hostess, "What is the one truth that's meant the most to you recently?"

She immediately said Deutoronomy 31:8.

Well, her reference was a verse tucked away in an OT Book teeming with violence and disobedience. I looked up the verse.

It was like drinking a cup of cold water in the desert.

It said, "The Lord himself goes before you and will be with you, he will never leave you or forsake you. Do not be afraid; do not be discouraged."

It was a message straight to my beleaguered heart.

I have been struggling with news from Ukraine, wrestling with a personal health issue, and generally feeling powerless.

I asked Chris, my hostess, 'Why did this verse move you so much?"

She instantly gave a simple answer: "Because it's the truth."

A cancer survivor herself, she had just sent this verse to a family member in the throes of the same disease.

It was so elegantly simple...pouring encouragment on my thirsty soul.

"Because it's the truth." .

Truth that rose above mayhem. Truth that set me free.

It was like God said to me "I said it. That settles it. Remember it."

Four times this small verse mentions "you". He's not only sovereign, He's personal.

He's in charge of all paths. AND has one perfectly designed for me and you.

Better yet, He goes before us on the Path. Forsaken or abandonment is not in His vocabulary.

And last, He gives two powerful commands—not suggestions--as we both walk the path.

Don't be afraid and don't be discouraged. Fear not and hold fast. I've got your back.

Here's the thing: it's so easy to forget it all when the storms are crashing. (John 20:29)

So when He says "I will never leave you nor forsake you" we have a choice. I choose to believe it's true.

When He says we are kept and secure …He means it. As the song says, "We're fighting a battle He's already won."

This truth has caused me to remember...

We are here by God's appointment.

In His keeping.

Under His training.

For His time.

Let's call it True Truth.

Wheelchair Questions

I've found there are two ways to ask questions.

One I would call "armchair questions" and the other "wheelchair questions."

Armchair questions are asked as though they've never felt suffering or pain. Or as Shakespeare wrote, "He jests at scars that never felt a wound."

Wheelchair ones say, "Let's be honest. Can we stop the pious nonsense that life goes well for good people and badly for bad people?"

Or "Why do so many who don't give a hoot about God seem to live happier, longer lives?"

The Book of Job asks it best, "Why do the wicked have it so good? (Job 21:7)

I've discovered that behind most front doors lurks pain, often hidden and drawn out, at times very deep.

So, wheelchair realists ask: "What kind of God runs a world like this?"

Enter the book of Job. A staggeringly honest book. A book about what people actually think—just not what they say in public—or ever ask in church.

Job is an old fireball book. It both unsettles us and calms us at the deepest level Forty two long chapters of no easy answers. No pat academics. No clever memes.

After a powerful beginning, there are loooong pauses in the Book. Why? Because in grief or suffeing there are no quick fixes. No self-talk phrases that work for long.

God speaks from His heart to ours. Job is His poem to us when things don't fit in our religious boxes.

Most new cities I have visited overseas start with a Hop-On, Hop-Off bus ride. A 90 minutes whirlwind of the touristy spots. Just give me the big picture--fast.

Job is no whirlwind tour. It is a Book to be experienced—not just studied. To be felt, absorbed in wonder, unsettled and pressed down.

Job challenges me to change my questions. Why? Because of one bold statement at the end.

God says, "No one can stop my purpose." (Job 42:2).

Think about it. Seriously? Those six words change everything.

I am forced to move from a coffee shop with a soft armchair to a hard wheelchair on a messy corner in Calcutta, or a trench in Ukraine.

In a world that increasingly doesn't make a lick of sense, I need to learn about Job. His bewidering world didn't make sense either.

So for the next couple of Salt Talks I will slug it out with a man named Job who was ushered into a chamber of horrors.

Not of his making either. And God clearly, purposefully, allowed it. (Job 1--3).

So if you're battling unrelenting pain, suffocating loneliness, or feeling the silence of God--like Job, one day you will--climb in your wheelchair.

I've got an open spot next to mine.

To Infinity and Beyond

It was the little known theologian Buzz Lightyear who said, "To infinity and beyond." Oh, out of the mouth of toys.

Not sure you can go beyond infinity, but infinity answers so many questions.

I used to compete in the broad jump in track. Granted it was in high school, but I still thought I was hot stuff: jumping all of 17 feet or so.

Then I read about one of the oldest track world records still standing: done 34 years ago at the World Championships in Japan.

Mike Powell of the USA soared a stunning 29 feet, 4 inches.

I use a spiritual analogy often involving a person trying to broad jump over the Grand Canyon.

Whether you can jump 17 feet or 29 feet, trying to jump it as a sinful person reaching a holy God, you'll still suffer the same fate: a big splash in the Colorado River.

Our works are never good enough. Or as someone said, "Since nobody's perfect, how good is good enough?" The answer is no one.

It takes Someone to bridge the 18 mile Grand Canyon gap. That Someone is Jesus. While the illustration makes the point, it still falls woefully short.

The chasm is really "to infinity and beyond." When I grasp a smidgeon of that, my God get's bigger, my questions become irrelevant, His grace becomes everything.

The resurrection of Jesus becomes my Mt. Everest. Everything else becomes mole hills.

When we read God "Casts our sin as far as the East from the West" it literally means FROM forever TO forever. (Psalm 103:12).

To put it another way, He takes our sin to the Vanishing Point. "I will remember their sin no more." (Hebrews 8:12)

It's why the Psalmist sings, "God is the Sovereign King of the Vanishing Point." What is that?

The Vanishing Point is when two parallel lines finally converge. It's also when our minds become mush.

How unfathomable. Exactly.

Some people a lot smarter than me try to answer impossible Grand Canyon questions. Some can broad jump 30 feet. The older I get, I feel victory jumping out of bed.

Questions like: "Why pray when God knows the outcome?" "Why share the Gospel when He knows who will come to faith?" "How could God die on a Cross?" On and on.

Or the biggest one of all: "How could God love a sinner like me?"

I don't know. I'll need to jump into an infinite eternity to find out. All of us will. And only belief in Jesus insures a soft landing. (John 6:47)

"For I am convinced that neither death, nor life, nor things present, nor things to come, no powers, nor height, nor depth, nor any created thing shall be able to separate us from the love of God." (Romans 8: 38—39). His inescapable, Immeasurable love.

Love to Infinity and Beyond.

Try broad jumping over that.

The Accuser

If you think it's bad now, hang on. It will get worse. Much worse.

There is an Invisible War going on around us.

Of all the major truths of the Bible it is the most neglected and least talked about.

It is the Spiritual War between God and Satan...who's also known as the Devil, The Father of Lies, the Prowling Lion, the Enemy.

Whatever you call him...he's a fallen angel bent on our destruction. He's real and his demon agents are after us.

Here's the one thing I know: he is the Accuser. He accuses us before God and accuses God before us.

So it was with God's servant Job. One of the most important verses in the Bible is found in Job, chapter one...when our Public Enemy #1 asks God a life changing question.

"Will Job serve You for nothing?" (Job 1:9)

Does Job, a righteous man, only serve You because you've been good to him? He's got if all: health and wealth, family and friends.

The devil says "if you take it all away, he will curse you to your face." Satan accuses Believers today in the same way: he thinks we serve God only because it's a good deal.

Our part in the God's Story, like Job's, is more important than we could ever imagine. I think God is looking for people who will still serve Him—no matter how tough it gets.

I believe every conceivable situation in which Satan can accuse a Christian will be presented before God.

If you have lost a child, find yourself homeless and broke, suffering thru a horrific marriage, enduring an incurable illness— YET continue to trust Him...God and HIs angels are taking notes.

Court is in session 24/7.

The devil, as our accusing prosecutor, brings up a million hellish examples of people in pain, loss, and disaster. And God, as our defense attorney, says. " David or Carol trusted Me with those exact problems."

Case Dismissed.

When Satan exhausts his list of awful scenarios, and after God finds a person who has served Him in spite of them— I think Jesus mounts His White Horse.

Which leads to THE question: Will you and I serve God for nothing? Satan is betting we won't. Our Heavenly Father is betting we will. What If we don't? He'll move on to find someone else.

The glorious truth is you may have the honor of ushering in the second coming of Jesus Christ.

Willing to lose it all and hold fast?
We didn't start the Invisible War.
We may hold the key to ending it.

Bought

The older I get, the more sappy I get. Three truths just make me teary.

Every time I think about the cry of Jesus on the Cross, "My God, my God why have you forsaken Me," I cloud over with emotion.

His broken fellowship within the Trinity was because of my rebellion. An empty tomb for the likes of me is incomprehensible.

I also have the same emotional meltdown when I think about Abraham and his son Isaac. How could a father put his only son on an alter of sacrifice and raise his knife to kill him?

I have a son. I simply could not do it.

But there is one more truth that causes a heartfelt cry. I realize I am entering the Holy of Holies now. It's a mind boggling mystery.

The Bible says, "You have been bought with a price. You are not your own. Your body is a temple of the Holy Spirit." (I Corinthians 6: 19--20)

My cracked pot of a body holds a transcendent Treasure--God Himself. (II Corinthians 4:7)

The Maker of the Universe lives inside every Believer. The Spirit of God now nests inside me. I am a walking Ark of the Covenant.

Full stop: Don't rush past that truth. Think about it...He lives inside of us. Pouring forth Living Water. Blows all of my fuses.

And as if that's not enough, we are not our own. He owns our bodies. He paid our ransom. HIs priceless blood was the cost.

It means He has full rights of ownership. Being His slave has, ironically, set me free. What does that mean?

If I have cancer, so what? My body is His. He can do whatever he wants with it—decaying and all. If He wants me to be on assignment with cancer, it's His choice.

Want a peaceful life? "I belong to Him. I have been bought". Play those two phrases on repeat.

No longer performing. No longer pretending. No longer promoting. No longer living like an unbeliever.

My biggest spiritual problem? I forget I have been purchased.

Our Father knew we were damaged goods. He bought us anyway. (John 3:16)

Our Jesus knew we were bent to evil. He bought us anyway. (John 3:16)

Our Spirit knew we were lost. He bought us anyway. (John 3:16)

He loved us enough to buy us for the price of Easter.

Does that fill you with thanksgiving? Overwhelm you with humility? Reignite you with wonder and praise? If not, pause and reflect.

OR when you ask "Where are you God when it hurts? Where are You when my groaning is too deep for words? Where are You when nothing makes sense?"

Pause and listen very closely. Lean in.

He'll whisper to His thirsty child...

"I'm right here, I bought you."

The Blood Never Lies

I turned 78 a week ago and I think the legendary Vince Scully, broadcaster for the LA Dodges for 67 seasons, was right.

Upon retirement he was asked what he was going to do now? He replied, "Get a smaller home and a larger medicine cabinet."

After 75, doctors tend to rule your life. My pill box is the largest one they sell.

I feel good but when they do that comprehensive blood panel, my list of maladies are 10 times longer than my to do list.

The secrets are found in the blood. It doesn't matter how good I feel. The blood never lies.

I was completing a week of teaching in India near the border of Nepal. There was a graduation ceremony on a Sunday and I was asked to speak.

Little did I know that part of my duties that day was to baptize new believers in the pond right next to the tiny chapel. Surprise #1.

After the ceremony, I took off my sports coat, unloosened my tie and waded out into the murky waters.

My second surprise...there were over 50 being baptized...with songs in between each immersion.

Three hours later I finished. My toes and fingers were wrinkled and I was exhilarated, exhausted and emotionally drained.

After the last one had been dunked, it was almost dark and I was ready to go to my hotel and sleep.

Except for one small detail. I was told the pond was infested with leeches and it was a certainty I had attracted baptismal companions. Surprise #3.

So in one of the most awkward post water baptisms in history I stripped and in the most vulnerable places...I was examined...my Indian host with a lighter in hand to pry the blood suckers off.

They didn't cover this in seminary.

Believe it or not...I'm thinking about my India experience as we enter Holy Week.

As squeamish as leeches are, I find myself reflecting on those little critters in India. Why? Because they are utterly dependent on the Blood.

Believers are too.

I'm overwhelmed with the thought of my Savior-God shedding His blood on the Cross. For me. For you.

The Bible says, "We have now been justified by His blood and saved from His wrath (Romans 5:9)."

"We have redemption through His blood, the forgiveness of sins (Ephesians 1:7)."

"You were redeemed by the precious blood of Jesus (I Peter 1: 18–19)."

The Lord's words are strong, "Whoever drinks my blood and eats my flesh inherits eternal life."(John 6:54). It's a call to discipleship.

It's a plea for Believers to get serious.

Jesus told His men during the Last Supper, "This is my blood poured out for the forgiveness if sins…drink it in memory of Me." He bids us to drink freely.

My physician takes my blood and diagnoses my life in this world.

It never lies.

The Great Physician gives me His Blood and promises Life in the next.

He never lies.

Sealed With A Kiss

I'll bet you can remember your first kiss. Good, bad or in between---it's impossible to erase.

The songwriter says, "A kiss is just a kiss." I beg to differ.

There are kisses on the cheek in Europe. Eskimos kiss nose to nose. We blow kisses to each other.

There are romantic kisses, family kisses, butterfly kisses.

You can kiss it goodbye. Seal it with a kiss. Or simply write "kisses" to say good night.

Last night, following dinner with friends, we were listening to random songs and up popped one of my favorites— powerful in any Season.

It's the song "Mary Did You Know?" These lyrics written to the Mother of Jesus melt me, "And when you kiss your little baby, you've kissed the face of God."

Did you know the Bible urges Believers to kiss God? In fact, it says we are at our most healthy and holy when we do.

The admonition is found only one place in the New Testament. The Greek word is proskuneo (John 4:23). It's a word connected to the deepest kind of worship. The means literally "to kiss God in worship."

It's expressing intimate joy. To love Him from your heart. not because you have to—but because you can't help it.

We kiss God when we run out of words. When all the singing, praying, praises move us to a whole new level. Why?

Because spiritual kisses are ultimately the most intimate.

I believe when you truly, immeasurably love someone, you often run out of words. Or need new ones. Kissing your loved one replaces words as your heart exults.

We all have experienced groaning too deep for words (Romans 8:26). A Divine Kiss is exactly the opposite. It is intimacy too deep for words. Unbridled joy.

A perfect picture of a tender relationship. It's adoring our Abba Father.

To me, It's impossible to picture Jesus not hugging others while on earth. Inconceivable that He will not hug us in heaven. Along with tender kisses.

Easter reminds us the tomb is empty. The word is out that the Word is out.

So now we can fully worship. We sing, pray, praise…and when we run out of words, we reverently kiss the Lord of the Universe.

We greet the Lover of our Souls with worshipful, intimate inexpressible joy!

And seal it with a kiss.

Get on the Bus

I love the story of the blind man who was asked by the Pharisees, "Who healed you on the Sabbath?" His reply was classic.

"I do not know His Name…all I know is once I was blind, but now I see." (John 9:25) In other words, He changed my life. Didn't ask His Name.

Wanna argue with that?

Every Believer's story is a miracle. Even if we don't understand the Resurrection, how to defend the Bible, or make sense out of the Big Fish swallowing Jonah.

This is what we do know: Jesus Christ has rocked our world. It may be all you know. It may be all you need to know.

Ten years ago I was finishing up work in Lviv, Ukraine. Two years earlier I had spoken in Lusk, a city located two hours away. Now I was returning to it.

A group of us had taught English classes there, inviting the community to attend. I finished the night by sharing the Gospel.

Fast forward.

My Ukrainian host was taking me to the bus station but got sick. He left a note at my hotel on how and where to buy a ticket.

I was met there by a huge line at the ticket window. After handing the lady my instructions written in Ukrainian, she quickly took the money and pointed to a looong line of buses.

I was suddenly lost without an English word in sight. It was almost time for the bus to leave. I boarded a bus headed to who- knows-where, hoping the driver could speak English.

Nope. Siberia here I come.

I sat down in a random seat and we were off. An hour into the trip, in the middle of no where, a guy sitting in front of me suddenly turns around.

He stares at me, then asks, "Are you Randy Marshall?"

I knew I was either being arrested by Interpol or this guy was in the Ukrainian mafia. It was neither. It was better than that.

He told me he had attended an English class two years earlier and heard a guy from Dallas, Texas speak. He thought I looked familiar.

After finding out I was going in the opposite direction, we got off at the next stop. He rode with me all the way to Lutsk.

We didn't talk deep theology. No heavy doctrine. We did talk about how I was traveling blind. And he gave me sight. Turns out he was traveling blind too. My story gave him new eyes of faith.

Just so happened he left work early that day. Just so happened he got on my bus with a last minute ticket. Just so happened he sat in front of me. Just so happened he had a great memory.

I have discovered nothing in life just so happens. God plays chess. He always wins.

There will come a point in every person's life you'll be totally lost. Going in the wrong direction.

The Rescuer will send someone to help. You won't know his name. But he'll know yours.

All you know is you were once blind and now you see.

Our part?

Get on the bus.

All In Good Taste

Last Friday was one of the greatest days of my life. I got my sense of taste back.

For over two weeks food tasted like cardboard.

I took a Covid test. Nope. I ate hot and spicy food. Tasted like hot and spicy cardboard.

It was the worst unwanted diet in my life. Blah.

I still think sight is the most precious sense. I have moved dead taste buds up on the list.

As suddenly as it left, one morning it came roaring back. I took it calmly. I just about broke two legs and one neck racing to the refrigerator.

I'm embarrassed to admit how much of my day revolves around tasty food.

About Day 3 of my fasting from anything pleasurable, I started dreaming about the good old days. Chips and hot sauce, hot fudge sundaes, cinnamon rolls, French fries and filet.

I cancelled my birthday gig because 5 dollar Burger King cardboard tasted like 120 dollar Ruth Chris steak cardboard.

So…what lessons did I learn? Other than I am an addicted foodie?

First, I am weak.. I admit it. I love the sensual delight of lasagna, burgers, tacos and anything chocolate.

Second, I am blessed to live with an abundance of food. Central Market and Trader Joe's bring me close to coveting.

Last, the phrase "Taste the Lord for He is good" (Psalm 34:8) has taken on new meaning.

I asked the Lord to teach me about the gift of food. Turns out, food is a big deal in the Bible.

From Communion to the Wedding Feast. From Feeding the 5,000 to the Last Supper. From feeding a depressed Jonah to savoring the Passover. Dinners with sinners. Fish with Saints.

I lead a ministry where our outreach is to box food for "Feed My Starving Children." All over the world food is coupled with sharing the Gospel.

We have a saying around our home, "Where there's food there's love."

Wanna share your faith with a neighbor? Bring out the cookies and coffee, appetizer and dinner.

I've been in countries where the chicken served had lived a long hard life. Not much meat on the bone. But there was delicious fellowship.

I've eaten food in China and Africa that defy common sense to Americans. From monkey to donkey to beetles and brains. Oh boy!

But any I would have gladly tasted during the last two weeks-- to simply sense again.

I think a large part of hell will be a cessation of all senses. No sight, hearing, taste, touch, smell.

My brief time in tasteless purgatory has taught me He is my Living Water, my Bread of Life, my Sweet Honey, my Cup of Wine. Food Theology 101.

Taste the Lord For He is Good.
And His menu specials are Divine.

When It Doesn't Add Up

I love food. And I love miracles. I really love food miracles.

One of my favorites happened when Israel was wondering in the wilderness.

Feeding two million people is no easy task. Even when fresh manna was delivered every morning, the Israelites complained about it.

Complaining about a miracle! Can you imagine? Of course you can.

So what does God do about their incessant whining? He sends meat for a month.

Moses does the math and says it's impossible. It doesn't add up. He and his nomadic Jews are in the middle of nowheresville.

One month of meat? How about one day? It ain't happening. Then it does.

Then there's the boy with his lunch bag of loaves and fish. Keep in mind it wasn't just 5,000. Those were just the men.

It was more like 20,000. Jesus turns to Philip and asks, "Where shall we buy bread for these people to eat?"

Philip, like me, would have said, "It's not happening. It would take more than half a year's wages to buy enough bread."

It ain't happening. Then it does.

This past week our church sponsored its ninth annual Church Leaders Conference. 3,500 pastors from 40 nations.

The staff planned for one year to pull it off. Bar-b-cue, bacon and eggs for breakfast, Chick Filet for snacks, on and on. All staff and a slew of volunteers on deck.

I thought of manna and fish. I'm picturing feeding 2 million and 20,000—not 3,500 with the monumental work of catering, setting up tables, room capacity, a rain storm, parking, entertainment.

How did they do it? It didn't add up. Then it did.

So here's my question. What do you do when the will of God doesn't add up? My experience is the will of God rarely adds up.

It's always beyond my ability and my resources. In other words, I cannot do it or I cannot afford it.

You know God wants you to take a job that pays less. He wants you to go on a mission trip, but you can't take the days off. You know God wants you to adopt a child but you can't afford it.

Here's what I've found: it's not my job to ONLY crunch the numbers. I begin to audit the will of God. There's no miracle in that.

When you add God to any equation, His output always exceeds your input. You have enough. Bring it to Jesus. Then wait for the miracle.

Got two fish and some bread? Bring it. Got a few cows for two million meat lovers? Put your cows on the altar.

It ain't happening. Then it does.

Give him your lunch. He'll give you a feast. With 12 baskets left over. (Matthew 14) It won't add up.

Give him your cows. He'll give you His cattle...grazing on a thousand hills. (Psalm 50:10). It won't add up.

Then it does.

The God of Commas

Some things in this life are irreversible. What's done is done. Some are embarrassing, some are heartbreaking.

I remember standing over the casket of my brother Jack, who died of an overdose of heroin at 22.

If you've been on the receiving end of divorce papers, get a 2 a.m. frantic call as a parent, or see a lab report confirming your worst fears—you know what I'm talking about.

I think that's exactly how Mary and Martha felt about their brother Lazarus. Four days in the tomb and it was over.

But enter Jesus. Some days God shows up. Some days God shows off.

Did you know that after Lazarus died, his feet were bound, arms tied to his body with linen, with over 100 pounds of preservatives packed on? Picture a Mummy in a full body cast.

I believe there were two miracles that day. Obviously, when Jesus defeated death. Second, when Lazarus hopped out of the tomb. No way he just walked out.

"The dead man came out, his hands and feet wrapped with strips of linen, and a cloth around his face." (John 11:44).

The seventh miracle in John's Gospel doesn't just mirror our Lord's upcoming resurrection. It reflects ours.

So often, God inserts my own name when I'm in a dark tomb, when I start to smell funny and He insists…"Randy come out!"

I love this quote: "Never put a comma where God puts a period. And never put a period where God puts a comma."

We assume death is a period. Not so.

Remember what Jesus said about his friend, "This sickness will not end in death." (John 11:4) What? He had been dead four days.

The key word is END. Mary and Martha put a period on death. Jesus inserted a four day comma.

Ever felt like God was a dollar short and a day late? Nonsense. The Sovereign Creator is right on time. His time. God always gets the last word.

Two little words can change our destiny: Martha's words to Jesus, "If you had been here my brother would not have died, BUT I know God will do whatever you ask." (John 11:21)

BUT is a comma.

When Jesus says to her, "I am the Resurrection and the Life...do you believe this?" (John 11:25) Her answer sealed her destiny: "YES."

YES is an exclamation point!

I believe with all my heart real life comes out of darkness.

A seed in the ground. A baby in the womb. Jesus in the tomb.

And then there's Lazarus. From mummy to miracle. Jesus is the God of commas.

Lazarus come out! Need a miracle today? Insert your name.

Ditch those grave clothes and hop on out.

Sleep Talking

I was standing in line at the Los Angeles airport checking in for my flight to Seoul Korea.

My assignment was simple. I was invited to speak to a congregation from the Yoido church, one of the largest churches in the world.

Suddenly I was literally yanked out of line at the airport and asked to accompany some stone-faced Koreans to their downtown Embassy.

Evidently, my face looked like a terrorist on a most wanted poster. To this day, I have no idea why I was chosen to be interrogated. It was all like a Grade B movie.

Whisked into a small room, I was questioned as to why I was going, asked questions about my family, and finally given instructions to write an essay about my life.

I knew one thing: I would miss my plane. And the next one departed the next morning.

After I was mysteriously released 3 hours later with no explanation or apology, I rebooked my flight and got a hotel room.

By my calculations, without another interruption, I would make it to speak one hour after touchdown. Oh my!

I decided to try and make it. After sleeping fitfully through the flight, it miraculously landed in Seoul on time. It's a long flight.

Through customs and out the door, I had about half an hour to get to the meeting, which took place outside on the side of a mountain.

I was exhausted. I nodded off in the cab, and as I got out of the taxi I saw the gathered crowd.

A sea of 100,000 Koreans were crammed together. They were praying as I took my seat. The Koreans pray a loooong time.

Well, guess what you do when you close your eyes during a marathon prayer? Jet lag, my sleepless night, a nerve wracking interrogation took me to la la land.

It was only a huge ringing bell, attempting to silence the praying multitudes, that startled me back to reality. I was half way comatose as I heard "Marshall" in the middle of my Korean introduction.

How bad was it? Let's just say the old joke about the pastor who dreamed he was preaching and woke up... and he was" is no longer funny.

I have no idea what I said. My hosts said later it was "exactly what they needed to hear."

Really? It's no wonder I believe in a miracle working God. When we are weak(or delirious), He is strong.

Like Balaam, he still speaks through a jackass. (Numbers 22: 21–39).

Here's what I learned that night: God works even when we sleep (Psalm 127:2).

Literally.

Put Your Hands Together

The choir had just performed beautifully with smiles as big as all outdoors. It was like angels we have heard on high.

They sang from their toenails during a chapel to a group of seminary students in Kyiv, Ukraine.

After three songs of foot tapping joy, the room of 50 or so students met their performance with dead silence. I was the only one applauding.

Everybody else just sat on their hands with faces that looked like Mt. Rushmore.

I recalled why seminarians are sometimes referred to as cemetery students. The frozen chosen.

I learned later the singing group had just been released from prison, became Christians behind bars, and this was their first performance.

I had arrived a couple of hours earlier...immediately asked to speak at the school's Chapel service before teaching a course.

I rose to speak after their performance. Nobody has ever accused me of being diplomatic. I asked the class to put their hands together for a stirring round of applause.

Crickets.

After I finished speaking, the President of the school said, "You might be wondering why we didn't applaud the singing group." The thought had crossed my mind!

He proceeded to tell me it was unbiblical to applaud others. He quoted Galatians 1:10: "Do not seek the applause of men, but the applause of God."

I was dumbfounded. I said, "That verse says we should not SEEK the applause of men. That singing group wasn't seeking anything. They were giving. And it's our privilege to give back."

It's called encouragement, kindness, hospitality and about 50 other ways Christ affirms people. The choir blessed us. We gave them the cold shoulder.

Put this up in flashing lights: People today desperately need encouragement. We die inside without it.

Teachers need it, moms need it, musicians need it, pastors need it. Dare I say If you're breathing —you need it too.

Far too often we become self appointed sin inspectors. God never gives anyone a critical spirit. I never had to go to school to learn how to be negative. Christian Curmudgeons.

"A word fitly spoken is like apples of gold in settings of silver." (Proverbs 25:11) We need loads of these precious metals in our rain-on-my-parade world.

Here's the truth: we know we are sinners. We know we are insecure and one step away from disaster. What we don't know is, "Do I matter? Am I enough?"

Our assignment? Go out of your way today to applaud our unsung heroes: Bedraggled moms. Drained teachers. Struggling pastors. Lonely kids.

What's the bottom line for Christians? We are God's appointed cheerleaders. We applaud God by applauding others.

So... let's put our hands together.

Give it up for _____.

Mark My Words

Do you think it was hard for Jesus to restrain His words when He was beaten, mocked, and whipped?

I think it's in the category of the Big Three Miracles: His conception, His resurrection and His ascension.

That He did NOT say anything is astonishing.

Legions of angels were at His beck and call with swords drawn. Ready to hear one word from Him.

His love triumphed over His power. When His love was at His highest, His power was at His lowest. By choice.

It's why we have a Savior.

To me, His power to perform 34 distinct miracles in the Gospels is awesome. But His willpower in NOT doing what He was capable of doing is equally amazing.

When I know I am "right" it is nearly impossible to keep my mouth shut.

Yet the Lamb of God was silent before His shearers. (Isaiah 53:7) The Creator of the universe uttered not a word before His Kangaroo Court.

Curse them? Instead, He said, "Forgive them, for they know not what they do." (Luke 23:34)

One writer put it this way, "It was love that led Jesus to the Cross. It was willpower that kept Him nailed there."

I've made my living as a speaker. Add being a husband, dad and grandfather and I know one thing: "In the power of the tongue is both life and death." (Proverbs 18:21)

Words create defining moments. Words can build up or tear down.

When my 4th grade teacher said to me, "Randy, I think you would make a good speaker" it changed the trajectory of my life. When my family said 7 years ago, "You ought to write, I started posting Salt Talks."

When my baseball coach told me my skills were mediocre at best to make it professionally, it stuck. I never rose above average.

Charles Spurgeon was upbraided one time for using too much humor in the pulpit. He replied, "You would commend me if you knew what I held back."

Hurtful words spread like fire: it doesn't take long to scorch a reputation. It's like unscrambling an egg. Damage is done. Sorta like putting toothpaste back in the tube.

But timely words can pierce like fire: igniting the heart with hope.

I've hurt people by lashing out, whispering innuendo, adding my opinion, talking too much.

But no one has ever been hurt by me shutting up or building up.

Mark His Words.

Or His silence.

The Will

I think truly holy people are down-to-earth people.

So let's get down to earth.

In the end, there are only two rules in life.

The rule of heaven is "Thy Will Be Done."

The rule of hell is "My will be done."

If you pray the former, be prepared to cooperate with the answer.

And here's the truth.

God always answers.

No, Yes, Wait.

Longing For IT

I am homesick for a place I've never been.

The Germans have a word for IT: farsickness.

IT's what C.S. Lewis called the "far off country."

I think all of us have IT…and we don't know what to call IT. Or how to satisfy this deep craving.

IT's a yearning for more. IT's a longing for our real home.

Unbelievers search for IT. Believers are on tiptoes waiting for IT.

IT's that undefinable, undeniable hunger.

Where every tear is wiped away. Where everything sad becomes untrue. Where reunions happen.

IT's when we get goose bumps, tear up and have nostalgia for places we only dream about.

Even if our minds deny IT—our souls cannot. IT'S to have things the way they ought to be.

IT's the stories and films that tap into our deepest desires, like Lewis' Chronicles of Narnia. Or Tolkien's Middleearth.

IT happens when we picture the Irish Coastline or the highlands of Scotland. Zion in Utah. Banff in Canada.

IT shows up when we see videos of a dad or mom returning from serving in the military? When they surprise their little boy or girl at school.

I almost cannot handle IT.

IT happened when our scrappy hockey kids beat up on the Russian pros for the Olympic Gold. IT happens when the humble are exalted.

IT happened when I visited a children's home in Arkansas for physically challenged kids. I remember pleading: "Thy Kingdom come…thy will be done…on earth as it is in heaven."

IT's an Eden do-over. IT'S Healing and restoration.

I think every person on earth feels IT because "Eternity has been set in our hearts." (Ecclesiastes 3:11)

The Germans call IT Farsick.

I just call IT Homesick.

He Knows

It usually hits me in huge airports.

As I walk through terminals like Hong Kong, Beijing or Istanbul, I pass thousands of people—scurrying to their gates.

I think, "God knows all of these people inside and out. Every thought, every problem. He knows all 8 billion people intimately."

So, I wonder, what's a big number to God?

The number of stars in the universe? He's named them all. Sand on the shores? He's counted them.

Birds of the air? His eye is on the Sparrow. Hairs on our head? He's numbered them. Thoughts in our mind? He knows before we think them.

Maybe 8 billion is a small number to God after all.

One thing's for sure: His thoughts are not mine. They are past finding out. Unfathomable. Unsearchable. (Romans 11:33-36)

I've stopped trying to unscrew the inscrutable. All I know is He knows, He sees, He feels.

I purpose to be like a child again. (Luke 18:16) I will rest in this: He doesn't miss a thing. Big or small. Texas floods or sleepless nights.

In Luke 8, a desperate woman has been suffering 12 years with a blood issue. In a crushing crowd, she touches the prayer shawl of Jesus. Power rushes out of Him and the woman is healed.

Jesus asks, "Who touched me?"

This socially rejected woman, avoided as unclean, falls to her knees and confesses. Jesus speaks tenderly to her, "Daughter, your faith has healed you. Go in peace."

He then calmly raises a 12 year girl from the dead. He takes the hand of the child and affectionately says, "My child…get up."

From the macro to the micro, Jesus Christ is forever involved. The Maker of the Stars calls us by name.

Transcendent and Tender. This is our Savior.

The first quote I framed on my wall as a new Christian: "When I cannot see His hand, I can trust His heart."

I believe it now more than ever.

The Helpers

One of my heroes was Fred Rogers. He had a way of calming me down.

I wish he had been around over the July 4th weekend. Things weren't so beautiful in the neighborhood.

In fact, the nightmare continues along the Guadalupe River in Central Texas.

No amount of Bible or Theology in this "time to weep" and "time to mourn" explains it. No logic untangles the incomprehensible.

Every Bible verse leaves me with more questions. Every bit of explanation leaves us cold. Let's face it, nobody has answers.

The mind rebels when we think the One who brought the rain could have stopped it. The One who raised the flood waters could have lowered them.

So let's move our theology from our head to our heart. And just feel these days. Words are such clumsy things when nothing makes sense.

Thank goodness for guys like gentle Fred Rogers. His whole life was dedicated to helping kids.

With so many children going to heaven during these days, somehow Fred has been God with skin on for me.

He made one statement that doesn't dry my tears, but causes me to feel another emotion besides anger and grief.

He said, "My mother said when there is a catastrophe to always look for the helpers. If you look for the helpers there's hope."

And helpers have indeed descended on a raging river that rose 26 feet in 90 minutes.

Coast Guard Helicopters flew in from Corpus Christi where rescue swimmers like Scott Ruskan moved 165 kids to safety.

Rescue boats have snatched kids from trees. Grief Counselors have gone to work. Volunteers from across the nation have brought supplies.

Our son in law raised thousands of dollars with a few calls and sent a chef with food feeding game wardens.

Camp leaders have desperately helped kids to higher ground. Some giving the ultimate sacrifice.

In the midst of hell look for the heroes. They are the helpers. Anguish is softened by the hugs of heroes.

Today, a community of fellow feelers rise to the occasion. Many are Believers. Believer or unbeliever, we weep and we help.

Songs have been written; poems of lament have been penned. Prayer became our first response. "Oh God…" our first words.

So instead of trying to understand, I have been asking God for a "peace that PASSES understanding." (Philippians 4:7)

Instead of searching for the Why's I have been looking for the Who's. The hands, arms and feet of Christ.

The Bible asks a question, "From where does my help come from?" The answer is clear, "Our help comes from the Lord." (Psalm 121)

A swollen River became a burial ground for perhaps hundreds of precious souls during these two weeks. They found their eternal hope complete: "Christ in You, the Hope of Glory."

For now we weep. In the face of death, so did Jesus. (John 11:35)

In this fallen world, we can become bitter, blame others, even rail against God. He can handle it. He also lost a Son.

Or I can find hope.

And look for His Helpers.